Designs for Relaxation and Mindfulness

MANDALA

HEART AND SWEAR WORD COLORING BOOKS FOR ADULTS

TEST YOUR COLOR

TEST YOUR COLOR

Shit

DOUCHE

Dipshit

Shit-a-brick

Fuck Off

Beaver
Dam

Fuckwit

LOVE

You
Dreams
We
Desire
I ♡ You
Love
I ♡ You

BASTARD

Love

Damn

Sugartits

Asshole

Fuck
Nugget

SUGAR TITS

www.ingramcontent.com/pod-product-compliance
Lightning Source LLC
Chambersburg PA
CBHW081414280526
45788CB00009B/3095
9781542588409